IMAGES OF
WORLD WAR II

IMAGES OF
WORLD WAR II

ALISON GAUNTLETT

Photographs by the
Daily Mail

This is a Parragon Book
First published in 2006

Parragon
Queen Street House
4 Queen Street
Bath, BA1 IHE

Produced by Atlantic Publishing

A catalogue record for this book is available
from the British Library.

ISBN 1-40544-895-4
Printed in China

ACKNOWLEDGEMENTS

The photographs in this book are from the archives of the *Daily Mail*.
Particular thanks to Steve Torrington, Dave Sheppard,
Brian Jackson, Alan Pinnock, Richard Jones and all the staff.

Introduction

World War II is a time which lives in the memory of many people: those who served in the fighting or on the home front and those whose lives were shaped in the world that followed the ending of the war. *Images of World War II* tells the story of the momentous conflict that scarred and fashioned the world we know to today.

Many of the events of that conflict, such as the D-Day Landings, the Blitz, the battles in North Africa and the Pacific are ingrained in the consciousness. *Images of World War II* captures those dramatic moments but also presents many other aspects of that conflict in a valuable testament to the all-encompassing nature of war.

Photographs from the comprehensive and assiduously maintained *Daily Mail* archive have been restored to their original quality to tell the story, not only of the fighting, but of how the war affected men, women and children in their daily lives. These rarely seen photographs, some never published at the time, vividly detail what life was like for ordinary people as they struggled with bombing, shortages of all essentials, the unremitting toil to keep the country going, and the ever-present sense of loss. But alongside these photographs are those that show the humour and defiance of the human spirit.

IMAGES OF
WORLDWARII

War is declared

Above: Hitler marched into Austria on 13th March 1938, thus making it part of the Third Reich; again in direct conflict with the terms of the Treaty of Versailles. He was determined to absorb a section of Czechoslovakia containing three million Germans into the Reich, claiming to Neville Chamberlain this would be his last demand for additional European territory. Chamberlain acquiesced but in March 1939, Hitler continued further into Czechoslovakia, also taking over Memel in Lithuania. Sensing that he would next look towards Poland, Britain signed a pact promising to assist Poland in the event of a German attack. The British Government was right and Hitler finally

invaded on 1st September 1939. Hitler ignored Britain's ultimatum and at 11.15 am on Sunday 3rd September 1939, war was finally declared on Germany.

Opposite: By 1934, Adolf Hitler had combined the titles of President and Chancellor, establishing himself as Fuehrer and renaming the Weimar Republic as the Third Reich. He had already defied the Treaty of Versailles by re-arming the country, and the German officers, after routinely swearing an oath of allegiance to Hitler, were frequently demonstrating their power and strength with military parades.

Preparations begin

Opposite: Many German and Czech refugees were among the crowds that gathered at Downing Street to hear the inevitable announcement as Prime Minister Neville Chamberlain declared, 'This country is at war with Germany'.

Above: Even before the declaration of war, everyone had been issued with a gas mask, thirty-eight million in total. In the early days of the 'Phoney War' people were very lax about carrying them and many ended up at lost property offices such as this one in Baker Street.

Gas masks made compulsory

Gas masks were designed to protect the public in the event of a poison attack and it was actually an offence not to carry one. Babies were issued with complete suits and Mickey Mouse designs were provided for children. Mussolini had used chemical weapons when he attacked Ethiopia in 1935 so everyone's fears were fully justified. Leaflets advised the public how to recognize the signs of gas by the smell of pear drops, geraniums or musty hay and the tops of pillar-boxes had been painted with a special paint that changed colour if exposed to gas. Wardens used hand rattles to alert everyone in the event of a gas attack.

Above: A policeman directing pedestrians and traffic during a gas practice in Richmond, May 1942.

Evacuation begins

The stark reality of the official evacuation process actually began on 30th August 1939, but even prior to that date, some anxious parents had begun moving their children to safer areas, sometimes as far away as Canada. School-age children had to report to their school where they were labelled and escorted by teachers to the local railway station, clutching only their gas masks and the few clothes they were capable of carrying. For many it was their first experience of being away from home and some endured journeys as long as twelve hours, arriving exhausted and surrounded by strangers. Pregnant women, disabled people and younger children accompanied by their mothers were also moved, the number in the first few weeks of war totalling nearly four million

Above: Two very young evacuees share the Nipper annual as they travel by train to Devon. Ironically, many children and adults returned home soon after the war started, during the period known as the 'Phoney War'. However, the retreat from Dunkirk in June 1940 and the subsequent start of the Blitz prompted alarm and further mass waves of evacuation. Those who had originally been sent to the south-east, which had been perceived as a safe area, were moved to the west when it became clear that the south-east was highly vulnerable to attack.

Changes in children's lives

Opposite: Robert Yoghill and William Williams from Islington soon had to learn new skills at Eileen Hocking's family farm in Cornwall. For many children, evacuation meant a completely new culture and way of life. Some children who lived in squalid conditions in inner cities were suddenly exposed to all that the countryside had to offer, while others moved from advantaged homes to remote farms with no running water or electricity. It was obviously an experience that had a huge impact on them and often caused major problems for the children and their host families.

Above: Initially, those who had been evacuated to coastal areas were able to enjoy their freedom playing on the beaches but this luxury was limited as gradually coastlines were covered in barbed wire to protect the public from mines.

New school term delayed

Above: Children at Maryville Road School in Leyton escorted down to the school air raid shelter for safety. Initially, the new start of term had been delayed by many weeks, as schools could not reopen until they had their own air raid shelter. Schools were only allowed to teach the number of children for which the shelter could provide safety, often resulting in a part-time shift system with many limited to half a day's schooling.

Opposite: Early in the London Blitz people sought shelter in London's Tube stations. At first the authorities discouraged it, worried that the public might develop a 'deep shelter mentality' but public pressure made them relent.

London prepares for attack

Signs of war were quickly seen across the capital. There was an air raid warning on the day war was announced, although this turned out to be a false alarm. Soldiers were soon to be seen marching through London as the National Service Act came into effect. Protection methods such as sandbagging and blackout measures aimed to protect people and buildings in the event of an attack.

Opposite: Barbed-wire fences obscure a view of the Houses of Parliament.

Monuments under cover

Opposite: Signs of war became increasingly evident throughout the capital. Eros was stored for safety and the remaining plinth sandbagged, then boarded up, in attempt to protect it from attack – this process was applied to many other London monuments.

Above: The statue of King Charles I, just across from Trafalgar Square is given full protection as the lions quietly stand guard.

'Dad's Army'

Opposite: As Germany marched into France, a radio broadcast on 14th May 1940, by Anthony Eden, Secretary for War, appealed for any able-bodied people between the ages of 15 and 65 to assist in a home defence scheme to help protect the country from German attack. It was to be a voluntary scheme initially known as the Local Defence Volunteers and within 24 hours, a quarter of a million men and women had joined. Many units included First World War veterans, too old to enlist, but eager to help fight for their country. The age of these men led to the units being affectionately called 'Dad's Army'.

Above: The Citizens' Army hold their first parade on Tooting Bec Common. This was an early initiative to provide a defence unit that would protect the Home Front.

Churchill's Home Guard

Local Defence Volunteer units were divided into zones linked to districts and counties, with some created from companies or public bodies, all under army command. On 23rd July 1940, at Churchill's direction, their name was changed to the Home Guard. Initially wearing civilian clothes and using antiquated weapons, the training and structure of the organisation grew throughout the war. Eventually there were 1.75 million members divided into 1,100 battalions.

Above: The Parliamentary Home Guard being inspected by Winston Churchill.

Opposite: Lord Strabolgi takes his duty turn on a snowy day in the Palace Yard for the Parliamentary Home Guard.

Aerial skirmishes

The Battle of Britain officially began on 10th July 1940. Aerial skirmishes were soon seen in the skies with the vapour trails signalling to those on the ground that fighter planes were in action.

Conscription of civilians

Even before the start of the war there was an obvious need to extend numbers in the armed forces. The National Service (Armed Forces) Act made all men between the ages of 18 and 41 liable for conscription although the Act did stipulate that single men would be called upon first. On 21st October 1939, men aged between 20 and 23 were required to register and this was then followed by a rather long process, as each age group was called, ending with the 40-year-olds in June 1941. By the end of 1939 just over 1.5 million men had been conscripted with 1.1 million joining the British Army and the rest divided between the RAF and the Royal Navy.

Opposite: A post-Dunkirk scheme encouraging men to get fit prior to joining the forces or home defence units.

Retreat from Norway

Above: By April 1940, Germany had invaded Denmark and Norway, finally forcing British troops to withdraw in the following month. This Lockheed Hudson was hit by anti-aircraft guns just prior to retreat but fortunately was piloted home with all the crew safe.

Opposite: At the start of the Battle of Britain, the Luftwaffe aircraft outnumbered the RAF by four to one, with the Germans using the Messerschmitt against the Spitfires and Hurricanes of Britain. The final number of aircraft eventually brought down by the end of the war totalled 915 RAF planes and 1733 from the Luftwaffe. One Messerschmitt, after being shot down, was towed past Westminster on its way to the scrap yard.

Luftwaffe under attack

Above: Officials surround a German plane after it crashed near the coast in north-east England.

Opposite: A German plane brought down in a farmer's field after a dogfight. Although the pilot survived and tried to escape, he was very quickly captured by the Local Defence Volunteers.

Italy attacks Libya

Above: Egyptian fighter pilots on a roll call. In September 1940, the Italian forces launched an attack on Egypt from their base in Libya. They moved fifty miles into Egypt, coming to a halt at Sidi Barrani. However as the Italians fortified the town, preparations were being made for a British counter-attack. General Wavell led the troops on 9th December and the town was successfully recaptured the next day. By the end of December, the Italian troops had been forced back into Libya.

Opposite: Egyptian guards seen at their posts, defending bridges and other strategic positions.

Britain prepares for attack

Above: Part of the preparations for the inevitable German invasion included the removal of signposts and street names. The aim was to make the country as difficult as possible for any invading German troops to move around. Plans were stepped up after the retreat from Dunkirk as the imminent danger increased.

Opposite: One of the first steps taken when war was declared was to fill and surround your house with sandbags, in the event of attack.

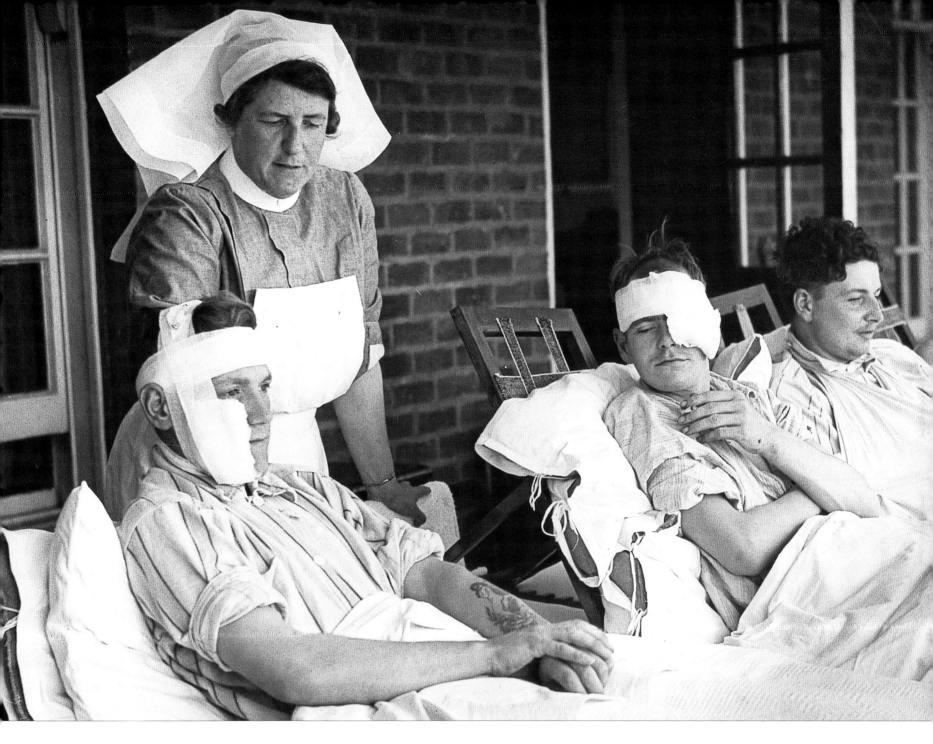

Troops return from Dunkirk

Opposite: On 10th May, Germany launched its Blitzkrieg against Belgium, Holland and Luxembourg. The Allies responded by directing their forces into Belgium, but as the German armies moved forward, the Low Countries finally fell with the Allied troops forced to retreat towards Dunkirk. The operation that was codenamed Dynamo, involved the rescue of 338,226 Allies from the beaches around Dunkirk between 26th May and 4th June, using any form of boat available on the English south coast. Although successful in saving lives, the loss of weapons and supplies was huge and Hitler gained control of the Channel coast in France. As men returned from Dunkirk, women and children were eager to greet them, offering food and handshakes. Many of the men had waited for hours and even days before being rescued and were given a hero's welcome as the trains passed through.

Above: A hospital in Hertfordshire was the destination for some of the soldiers wounded at Dunkirk.

Winston Churchill takes charge

After Neville Chamberlain had declared war on Germany he came under great criticism for the concessions he had made to Hitler, which people believed led to the inevitable outbreak of war. After Germany invaded Norway and Denmark in April 1940, Chamberlain finally bowed to pressure from his own party and resigned on 8th May. Two days later, Winston Churchill took over as Prime Minister, leading a coalition government and also acting as Minister of Defence, leading the War Cabinet. His first task was to manage the retreat from Dunkirk and reassure the British public that England could fight alone. On 17th June he made an inspirational speech to the nation reassuring everyone of the strength of the armed forces and home defences saying, 'We will fight on, if necessary for years'.

The strength and might of the Hurricane

Opposite: Newspaper tycoon, Lord Beaverbrook, had been appointed head of the newly created Ministry of Aircraft, just prior to the start of the Battle of Britain. He immediately increased production and made a far-sighted decision to focus on fighter planes rather than bombers, which proved to be exactly what the RAF required in the summer and autumn of 1940.

Above: Hawker Hurricane aircraft in flight. By the start of the Battle of Britain, the RAF had a total of 2,309 of these aircraft in 32 squadrons. They were ultimately responsible for taking out more Luftwaffe planes than any other forms of defence.

The agility and speed of the Spitfire

Above: The Spitfire, designed by R. J. Mitchell and powered by a single Rolls-Royce engine, was renowned for its agility and speed. It could fly at high or low altitudes, was able to evade most enemy fighters and also performed valuable reconnaissance work. During the war 'Spitfire Funds' were set up, when groups would fundraise for a Spitfire to be manufactured. This was combined with public collections of donated metal such as aluminium pans. By the close of the war 20,351 planes had been produced for the RAF.

Opposite: A production line for the Miles Master, one of the RAF training aircraft.

The Home Guard protects Buckingham Palace

Above: On 20th May 1941 and again on 20th May 1943, the Home Guard was given the privilege of mounting guard at Buckingham Palace. This was an honour that many regiments had never been awarded despite being in existence for hundreds of years. Here, the Home Guard are seen marching through the gates of Buckingham Palace to take up their position.

Opposite: The Home Guard at Worcester Park inspected by King George VI, their Colonel-in-Chief.

Douglas Bader

Squadron Leader Douglas Bader was one of the RAF's most famous and renowned pilots. During a low-level aerobatic display in 1931, he had crashed and subsequently had both legs amputated, one above and one below the knee. He had prosthetic legs fitted but retired from the RAF, re-joining when war broke out. Bader flew with No. 242 Squadron, RAF Fighter Command and by the summer of 1941 had shot down 23 German planes. In August 1941, he collided with another aircraft over Le Touquet, was captured and remained in the Colditz prison until the end of the war.

Opposite: Pictured with Pilot Officer W. L. Knight (right) and Flight Lieutenant G. E. Ball (left) having been awarded the DSO (Distinguished Service Order) just after the Battle of Britain ended.

'Ginger' Lacey

Opposite: James 'Ginger' Lacey became one of the highest-scoring pilots of the Battle of Britain, bringing down a total of eighteen planes. Initially a member of the Royal Air Force Volunteer Squad, he joined the RAF when the war broke out. He flew Hawker Hurricanes and famously brought down the Heinkel He 111 plane that had bombed Buckingham Palace on 13th September 1940. He was then promoted to Flight Lieutenant and converted to flying Spitfires. Despite having been shot down or forced to land nine times, he successfully survived the war and by the time it was over, his final tally was twenty-eight planes destroyed and nine damaged.

Above: A bomber crew rest on a tender of bombs. These were soon to be loaded onto the aircraft behind, to be dropped over Germany.

On target

Opposite: Two barrage balloons brought down on 1st September 1940, after being shot by Messerschmitt 109s. One of the Messerschmitts was eventually brought down by rifle fire from the balloon crew afterwards. The barrage defences were raised into the air to deter low-flying bombers.

Above: As two Dornier planes flew over a target during the Battle of Britain, another aircraft photographed them from above.

Salvaging aircraft

Any German aircraft shot down were always stripped so any parts and the resulting scrap metal could be used to manufacture more British planes.

Opposite: Two workmen pause for lunch while stripping down the cockpit of a crashed Luftwaffe plane.

Above: Wreckage from a German plane that had fallen into a Kent garden in August 1940.

War heroes

Opposite: 'Al' Deere was a New Zealander who had a very distinguished war record. He served throughout the conflict often having to bale out of his own aircraft, but ultimately downed seventeen German planes.

Above: A large part of the life of a fighter plane crew was spent waiting to be called up for action. Ways of passing this time would include sleeping, listening to the gramophone or radio or on this occasion, a game of chess.

Battle of Dover Straits

During the summer in 1940, the Channel witnessed endless land and sea battles. The Germans had long-range guns sited on the French coast with the shellfire sometimes reaching Dover. Small barrage balloons known as kite balloons would be raised over convoys to try to avoid dive-bombers or low-flying swoops. The supplies the convoys brought in from abroad were vital to Britain and were often subject to attacks from mines and U-boats as well.

Above: A photograph taken from the cliffs at Dover shows a convoy under attack from the French coast.
Opposite: The puffs of smoke in the sky mark where anti-aircraft shells are bursting around the German planes which have just dropped bombs. On this occasion the bombers missed their targets making a hundred-foot-high waterspout.

Royal Naval Patrol Service

The Royal Naval Patrol Service was mobilised in August 1939 with its Central Depot based in Lowestoft. The depot became known as HMS *Europa* and provided the administrative headquarters for 6,000 vessels and 70,000 men. During World War I, it had been realised that small vessels were very useful for duties such as minesweeping and many fishing fleets had joined the Royal Naval Reserve. Their main role in the Second World War was anti-submarine work and minesweeping, initially around the British Isles. Their aim was to constantly minesweep the area to keep the shipping lanes clear, allowing the passage of convoys that were providing supplies.

Opposite: Semaphore being used to guide a merchant ship through a known minefield.

The Blitz begins

September 1940 saw the start of the Blitz, a nine-month-long bombing campaign by the Luftwaffe. It was Germany's aim to cause so much death and destruction that British people would urge the government to make peace with Germany. The bombing began in earnest during the day on 7th September when hundreds of incendiary bombs were dropped over the docklands area of London with the subsequent fires providing a guide for the night attackers. The East End was repeatedly bombed during the night and by the following morning 430 were dead with 16,000 injured. London was then repeatedly bombed, mainly at night, for the next 55 days. Burlington Arcade (above) and Regent Street (opposite) were just two London sites to suffer damage. Although bombing began in the docklands, the carnage soon spread across the city.

Air raids

On 18th September both John Lewis and Peter Robinson's department stores were completely gutted by fire after a night raid. The Inner Temple library, County Hall and several other major shops were also bombed that night.

Underground used for shelter

On the fifth night of the Blitz, Liverpool Street and a few other underground stations were used by East Enders to try to get away from the bombing raids. Unlike many others, they had no gardens in which to build an Anderson shelter and they were very wary of the brick street shelters. The underground not only provided safety but peace and quiet after a succession of sleepless nights. The government tried to discourage this at first, but it soon became clear that the trains could still run despite the crowds. The public would queue from early afternoon to get the best spaces and there was an official timetable to allow trains to continue to run: two yards of platform space were left for passengers until 7.30 pm, then one yard until 10.30 pm. The current was then switched off so spaces between rails could be used. By January 1940, after an initiative from Herbert Morrison, the Home Secretary and Minister of Home Security, bunks were being installed and tickets could be obtained for specific bunks. Snacks and sanitary facilities were provided and Swiss Cottage even had its own newspaper printed. At its peak 177,000 people were sheltering in seventy-nine stations.

The morning after

Police were often first on the scene, taking charge, directing people to safety and co-ordinating rescue services. After a daylight raid (opposite), a policeman had to climb up to check whether gas was leaking from this street lamp. Fires and gas explosions after bomb attacks were a constant hazard and the Civil Defence along with members of the general public needed to be continually vigilant.

Bombers attack transport links

The nightly attacks soon affected transport in the capital. Main line stations were frequently bombed with Southern Railway the most affected. Trains would often terminate unexpectedly and it became a daily task for commuters to find new routes to get to work. Buses were frequently diverted due to the danger of unexploded bombs. Those damaged were replaced with vehicles borrowed from other parts of the country and consequently had completely different colour schemes.

Opposite: A row of taxis was destroyed outside the Automobile Association's offices in Leicester Square. The lorry from the 'Gas Light and Coke Company' was on the scene to prevent any more damage from gas explosions.

Above: A tramcar destroyed during a daylight raid in Blackfriars Road.

Builders recalled from army

In October 1940, the government decided to release 5,000 building workers from the armed forces to try to repair the bomb damage. By this time 76,000 homes had either been destroyed or were uninhabitable. 250,000 people had been made homeless (albeit some only temporarily) and local authorities had only been able to rehouse 7,000. They had provided Rest Centres but these were severely overcrowded.

Opposite: Despite losing the complete wall of one side of this house, the interior remains largely intact – even the mirror on the wall survived.
Above: A fighter-bomber brought down in a London street.

Auxiliary Fire Service

The Auxiliary Fire Service was initiated to support the existing fire services during the extensive bombing campaigns. The service consisted of 60,000 members who would work a rota of 48 hours on, 24 hours off, which left many fighting for 40 hours at a time while bombing raids continued. The death and injury rate was extremely high. At times pumps were brought in from neighbouring areas but hose couplings did not always match other authorities' hydrants, which highlighted the need for standardisation in the future. A favourite German tactic was to send down incendiary devices and then attack the water mains to limit the supply of water to the fires.

Above: The Wolverhampton Auxiliary Fire Service demonstrates the power of one hundred hoses blasting water simultaneously.

Opposite: Fire crews clearing up after fighting blazes all night.

Buckingham Palace hit

Despite the ever-present dangers, the Royal Family lived at Buckingham Palace throughout the Blitz, enduring several attacks.

Above: Winston Churchill joined King George VI and Queen Elizabeth to inspect some damage in the grounds. The culprit was a time bomb dropped by a German raider. The area affected was part of the building adapted to provide a swimming pool for Princess Elizabeth and Princess Margaret.

Opposite: A crater just outside the gates was one of five, all caused by bombs dropped near to each other.

The Royal Family boosts public morale

Opposite: During a tour of London's East End, the King and Queen visited the site of a bombed London hospital. She praised highly the hospital staff, many of whom had been bombed out of their homes, continuing to work long shifts.

Above: Providing a reassuring presence, the Queen talked at length to East Enders who had endured a long night of bombing.

New roles for women

Prior to the start of the Second World War, most women were at home without any paid employment. In January 1940, Churchill asked women to help with the war effort which usually meant working in the munitions factories. In December 1941, women aged 20 to 30, with no specific responsibilities in the home were conscripted to either the forces or industry. As with men the age of conscription was gradually raised and even those needed in the home often took on part-time work. The roles undertaken varied from factory work, food production, and fulfilling tasks normally carried out by the men who had been called up.

Opposite: Volunteer ambulance women at their station in north-west London preparing for a practice run.

Above: A team of five female demolition workers take a break after pulling down a bridge over the LNER line in Wembley.

Coventry Blitz

Other British cities were also subject to devastating bombing attacks. On 14th November 1940 the medieval city of Coventry was virtually destroyed by the fires that raged after a night of vicious bombing. In total 568 people were killed with 863 suffering from serious injuries and the city was left with no transport or water supply. 449 bombers attacked Coventry dropping 10,224 incendiaries and 48 small, high-explosive devices, with the fires providing beacons for the bombers. The Luftwaffe's aim was to target the factories but as these were in residential areas, people's homes bore the brunt of the brutal attack. Although the main body of the cathedral was destroyed, the spire survived and towered triumphantly above the devastation.

Liverpool 'Christmas Raids'

Above: Between August 1940 and January 1942, Liverpool was constantly under attack. It was the most important port outside London and as a result of raids on the London docks, became even more essential. A vital route for military equipment and supplies, it was also home to many munitions factories. During this period a total of 4,000 people were killed and 3,500 seriously injured. Liverpool and Birkenhead were attacked on 20th and 21st December resulting in 365 people losing their lives. Forty-two were killed after bombing attacks on two air raid shelters and another 42 were killed after railway arches being used as unofficial air raid shelters were hit. 1399 children were evacuated out of the city.

Opposite: A child, a nun and a parishioner pray amongst the bombed-out wreckage of a London church.

Houses of Parliament hit

Above: Richard the Lionheart managed to survive an attack on the Houses of Parliament although his sword was not so lucky.

Opposite: During a twelve-hour raid by 413 aircraft in December, bombs hit the Houses of Parliament, causing damage to Cloister Court. The Member's Cloakroom is to the left of the guard.

A helping hand

Above: Salvation Army workers were on hand to provide tea to victims of bomb damage. It was up to the occupants to salvage as much as they could from their homes.

Opposite: This bus was damaged by the falling masonry during a bombing raid.

'Second Fire of London'

On Sunday 29th December, a night of bombing dubbed the 'Second Fire of London' took place after hundreds of incendiary bombs set off a series of massive fires. 136 planes dropped 22,068 firebombs and 127 tons of high explosives. The Germans had deliberately chosen a night when the Thames was at its lowest ebb, aiming their first bombs at the water mains. A total of 20,000 regular and auxiliary firemen fought the blaze.

Above: This remarkable photograph shows St Paul's Cathedral standing defiantly amongst the surrounding mayhem. St Paul's remained unscathed at the end of the war despite being subject to many bombing attacks. One device hit the building and lodged in the foundations but never actually exploded.

Opposite: On the Monday morning, clerks were helped by soldiers to salvage books from their offices. Much time was subsequently spent reconstituting records.

The aftermath

Above: A man surveys the debris after eight churches designed by Christopher Wren, the Old Bailey and three hospitals were set on fire and the Guildhall was badly damaged.

Opposite: The Lord Mayor of London spent New Year's Day 1941, inspecting the damage in Aldermanbury.

All clear

Above: A quick and effective method for the police to give the 'All Clear'.

Opposite: Some residents in Plymouth remained undaunted as they gathered round a salvaged piano for a song; they had been bombed for three nights in succession.

'Business as usual'

Opposite: The scene at St Bride's street in London after a raid. The majority of the people were on their way to work and would need to salvage what they could from the premises and find alternative places to work.

Above: A company forced to leave their offices during a raid, continued their work in the open-air, complete with steel helmets for protection.

Pioneer Corps

Above: The Pioneer Corps was formed to help with clearance and salvage operations with the workers largely drawn from the unemployed. The Salvation Army was again on hand to provide food and drink for them.

Opposite: The Bank tube station was the site of the largest bomb crater in London, caused by a direct hit on 11th January 1941, killing over fifty people. A temporary bridge was built over the damage. In the original newspaper photographs the censors had blacked out the crater.

Strange surroundings

Opposite: The force of the blast at Grose's sports shop, New Bridge Street had forced several bicycles into the air leaving them strangely suspended from the wreckage.

Above: A new view of St Paul's is revealed from Queen Victoria Street after vast bombing damage and subsequent demolition.

A royal visitor

Above: The Duke of Kent (centre) seen inspecting bomb damage. He was an RAF pilot and was killed later in the war.

Opposite: A bomb dropped in April 1941 causes a crater in the north transept of St Paul's.

Rationing comes into force

The first food rationing came into effect in January 1940 and included items such as milk, meat, sugar and butter. Other items were also often in short supply. As the war progressed other foods such as tinned fruit were included under the 'points' system which at least allowed people to purchase luxury items occasionally. Shoppers had to register with a particular shop and could only buy rationed goods from there.

Above: All those with a surname beginning with 'A' were called to the Fulham office to register for new ration books.

Opposite: Queuing came to be a necessary part of shopping during the war. A long queue had formed outside a fish shop in Hammersmith with the customers needing to bring their own paper to wrap purchases.

Salvaging possessions

Above: A family occupy themselves as they wait for the removal van that would transport their belongings salvaged from their bombed-out home.

Opposite: An area close to St Paul's that was closed to the public and used to store materials needed to make buildings safe and subsequently rebuild them.

On the tent is printed: **LIFEBUOY EMERGE...** ... **HOT BA...**

Help for the homeless

Above: Lever Brothers were instrumental in providing hot baths along with free towels and soap for homeless children.

Opposite: Families gather in the street as they sit surrounded by whatever they can salvage.

Soldiers on leave

Left: A soldier pauses at a London station, laden down with weapons and equipment.

Opposite: A soldier is greeted by his delighted family as he begins ten days' leave.

Hospital targets

Hospitals were frequently a target during the bombing raids. In the clear-up operations, everything possible would be rescued, cleaned and reused. In this south-east London hospital four wards were completely wrecked but fortunately no patients were injured.

Opposite: Hatfield House in Hertfordshire was taken over by the government and used as a military hospital.

Sheffield hit

Opposite: The city of Sheffield suffered from a severe attack on 12th December 1940 which destroyed thirty-one tramcars and damaged nearly all the remaining stock. Sheffield United's Bramall Lane stand was also hit during the raid.

Above: A Dornier which had just machine-gunned streets in a coastal town was finally brought down on a beach. South-east England was known as 'Hellfire Corner' when it initially suffered from daily attacks. Eventually the Germans changed tactics and focused their bombing raids on major cities.

Luftwaffe airmen captured

Captured German airmen escorted through a London station in October 1940; they would be taken by rail to a Prisoner of War camp.

Any old iron?

Above: Metal was obviously an essential material needed to make munitions and consequently there was a huge drive by the government to encourage the public to donate structures such as railings. They would then be resmelted and sent to the munitions factories. These particular railings were dismantled from the play area used by Princesses Elizabeth and Margaret. During the course of the war the public donated nearly one-and-a-half million tons, which was sufficient to build 50,000 tanks.

Opposite: Hull was subject to constant bombing during May 1941. The city continued to be attacked during the following summer months. During one raid in July 1941, extensive damage was caused in New Bridge Road, a residential district.

Collecting paper and cans

Above: Norway, which was Britain's principal source of wood pulp to make paper, had fallen in May 1940. As a result all waste paper was gathered together by the public and then used for pulping. Over a million tons was collected in four years. No-one was allowed to use paper unnecessarily and toilet paper was in constant short supply.

Opposite: There was a huge drive to collect cans to reuse the metal and in East Ham alone the Borough Corporation was collecting twenty tons per week.

Improvements to Anderson shelters

Above: A new type of bunk for the home-based Anderson shelters was initially designed and made by a London policeman. The Ministry of Home Security then adopted and used the idea.

Opposite: During the twenties and thirties, no government money had been spent on armaments, so when war broke out, as well as the need for the raw materials, it was also essential to manufacture weapons as quickly as possible. This factory was working round the clock to produce the necessary small arms, tools and spare parts.

Women in munitions factories

Opposite: Women manufacturing 'Sten' guns at the Royal Ordnance factory in Theale, Berkshire. 'Women of Britain – come into the factories' was one particular recruitment slogan. Those working with munitions tended to make the casings for bombs and bullets and hence often worked with smelting furnaces and hot metal. These women would wear a beret and a cloak of undyed silk and rubber galoshes. Anything containing metal, even corsets, had to be removed in case a spark set off an explosion.

Above: Lilian Nye who had originally been a waitress was responsible for hauling a 500lb bomb on a crane.

Explosives factories sited out of town

Due to the overwhelming demand, all kinds of buildings including sheds were turned into mini-factories. The shells were often manufactured in the towns or cities and then sent to munitions factories situated further out to be filled with explosives. This reduced the loss of life in the event of an accident or enemy attack.

Above: Shells being readied prior to transfer to a filling shop.
Opposite: A production line for the Blenheim bomber. This aircraft was used in the early part of the war, often designated for very dangerous low-level raids, particularly against shipping targets. Due to the nature of its missions, losses were very high. It was withdrawn in 1942.

New ship-building techniques

Above: A new ship-building technique had been developed with this vessel being one of the first to be manufactured in this way. Britain had adopted a method used in the USA where the different parts of the ship were made at inland factories and the vessel was then assembled on the slipway at the shipyard.

This dramatically speeded up the manufacture of both merchant and warships and aimed to produce a battleship each week. Even as one was launched workers would be behind it preparing the slipway for the next.

Opposite: A production line in the Midlands making anti-aircraft guns.

'Lend a hand on the land'

The 'grow more food' campaign began at the start of 1940, coinciding with the beginning of rationing. As a means of increasing each family's food supply, people were encouraged to grow their own crops.

Opposite: These allotments were developed on one of the many bombsites in the City and tended by the firemen of the Redcross Street Fire Station.

Above: Children evacuated to South Wales helped with the potato harvest.

Public places used to grow crops

Aircrews were sometimes used to prepare land for planting as they had surplus time while they waited for their next mission. In March 1940 'Dig for Victory' Sunday saw people working on the land throughout the country. A significant amount of land was reclaimed during the war and the total amount of arable land available for farming crops increased by about 200%.

Opposite: Vegetable plots being tended in the shadow of the Albert Memorial in Kensington Gardens in London.
Above: Hurlingham Polo Club allowed Fulham Borough Council to use their grounds rent-free for allotments.

Allotments

Marches held during Women's Allotment Week. By 1943 nearly one-and-a-half million allotments were being tended.

Women's Land Army

The Women's Land Army actually began in 1917 during the First World War. Formed by Roland Prothero, the Minister for Agriculture, at that time there were 260,000 women working on the land. The organisation was then reformed in 1939 and numbers during the war were increased by conscription, so eventually there were 80,000 women working by 1944. Each county had its organising secretary and local representative who were responsible for ensuring that the women were content and that conditions of employment were being met. The days were long and the work was often gruelling; women were either billeted at private homes or housed in hostels. For many city dwellers there was a huge change in lifestyle that led to much homesickness. However, a great deal of camaraderie existed amongst the women and local dances were a much-needed source of entertainment. Tin helmets were often worn to protect them from debris when the RAF fighters brought down flying bombs, and they would regularly take shelter during battles.

Churchill

Opposite: With familiar cigar, Churchill salutes after returning from a review of the troops in the Middle East in 1943.

Above: Broadcasting to the nation wearing his 'siren suit'.

Unexploded bombs

Opposite: A caller to some newspaper offices in a London street is redirected. Unexploded bombs also caused disruption when buildings would need to be evacuated temporarily. The Bomb Disposal Section of the Royal Engineers was responsible for defusing unexploded bombs, a role that put them in danger on a daily basis. The drivers of one particular vehicle had attached a hand-written note at the back which read 'Suicide Squad'.

Above: As there were so many men serving in the forces women were often required to take over traditional male roles. Women 'navvies' carried out tasks such as shifting stones and were also involved in the much-needed demolition and construction work.

Adjustments to daily lives

Above: On the home front everyone regularly needed to make adjustments to their daily lives. With petrol in short supply and with constant disruption to public transport, buses were in greater demand so seats were removed to allow more standing room.

Opposite: Clothes rationing came into force on 1st June 1941 with the public issued with coupons to buy clothes. The 'Make do and Mend' campaign encouraged everyone to be thriftier with their existing clothes. Initially everyone had an allocation of sixty coupons although this was eventually reduced to forty-eight.

Americans join the war

America had adopted a neutral position at the start of the war, although giving economic and moral support to Britain. However, this all changed on 7th December 1941 when following an attempt at negotiations Japan launched a massive attack on Pearl Harbor, the American military base on the island of Oahu in the Pacific. No warning was given and as a result 188 American planes were destroyed with 162 damaged, 18 US vessels were sunk, 2,403 Americans were killed and 1,178 injured. All this happened in less than two hours. Britain and America declared war on Japan the following day. The first American

soldiers landed in Britain in January 1942. The name 'GIs' came from 'General Issue', a title referring to their kit and uniform. They sometimes had a reputation for being 'overpaid, oversexed and over here' but they were generally popular, especially with the women!

Above: An American soldier and a British WAAF enjoying the Whit Bank Holiday Fair at Hampstead in 1942.

Opposite: A British ATS with an American sailor at Speakers' Corner in London.

Petrol rationing

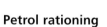

Right: Petrol rationing was introduced as soon as war broke out with the initial ration being three gallons per week. It immediately made people put their cars into storage for the duration of the war and halted the majority of motor sales. Instead the public walked, used public transport or bicycles.

Opposite: A hairdresser's in the West End of London the morning after a raid seen broadcasting the traditional words 'Business as usual'. It became a morale-boosting wartime slogan and was usually accompanied by Union Jacks.

'Tricycle girls'

Above: Again adjustments were made to traditional transport methods as the 'tricycle girls' delivered towels from a laundry service to City offices.

Opposite: The Brighton trolley bus conductresses achieved an absentee record of less than one per cent setting a national record for regularity. They would climb up and down the stairs an estimated 480 times in an 8-hour shift.

Baedeker Raids

The Baedeker Raids took place from April 1942 to the end of June. The name came from Baedeker travel guides of Britain as the public believed that this was how the targets were selected. Instead of attacking the industrial towns and cities, suddenly all the picturesque tourist cities such as Bath, Norwich, Exeter, Canterbury and York became targets. They did not have the air defences of the larger cities and consequently 1,637 were killed with 1,760 injured. Over 50,000 homes were lost. It was believed that these raids were in response to the Allied bombing of Lübeck in northern Germany. It had been a target as a base used to supply German troops on the Russian front.

Above: Four children drinking tea outside the remains of their home in March 1943.

Opposite: American troops wade ashore at Arzeu after using landing craft to get from ship to shore. As part of the North Africa campaign the 'Torch' landings began on 8th November 1942 with troops moved to Casablanca and Safi in Morocco and to beaches at Oran and Algiers in Algeria. The Allies were able to close in on the Axis armies, pushing them into Tunisia.

Above: The new remote-control chin-turret provided crew of the B17 Flying Fortress with better protection against frontal fighter assaults.

Opposite: Under the command of Lord Mountbatten the British troops in Burma were reinforced both on the ground and in the air carrying out some very successful campaigns against the Japanese. This scout group in the Burmese jungle included American, Chinese, British and native Kachin troops.

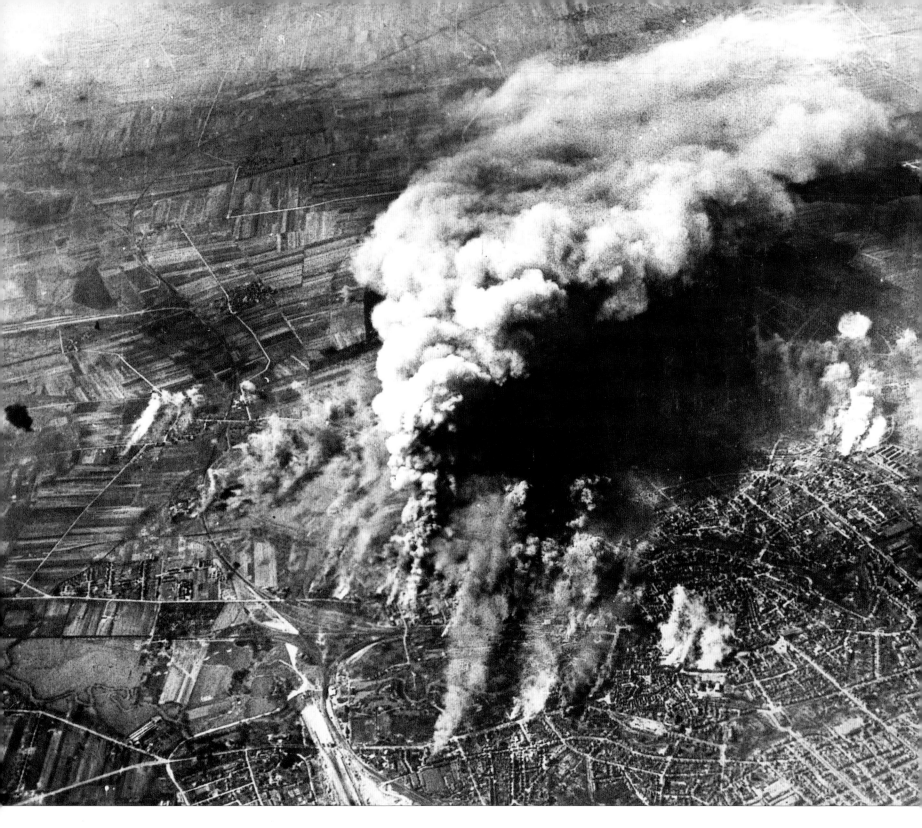

Attacking Germany

The autumn of 1943 saw massive air raids on Berlin by the Allies. It was the theory of Air Marshal 'Bomber' Harris that constant attacks on German cities would finish the war. However, the penalty was that in a four-month period the Allies lost over 1,000 bombers and their crews.

Above: An airfield and factory in Berlin ablaze after a bombing attack.
Opposite: Captured German prisoners carry an injured fellow soldier while being supervised by GIs. They were ultimately destined for detention camps in Britain.

D Day: Allies attack Normandy

Prior to the attacks on the Normandy beaches, 6th June 1944, bridges and rail links had been bombed which helped prevent the Germans getting to the front line. This, combined with the parachutists and gliders that took key points by surprise, made Operation Overlord a great success. By midnight the Allies had moved 155,000 men several miles inland, albeit with 9,000 losses. While the Allies embarked on days of hard fighting measures were put in place to allow a continual source of supplies and troops to the front line.

Opposite: These three German prisoners were marched out of the industrial town of Colombelles; it had fallen after heavy bombardment from the air.

Above: A German soldier surrenders to an American GI.

Advancing through France

By July 1944, the British troops had marched into Caen. However, the German army there held out, resulting in some ferocious bombing attacks. The city was finally liberated on 20th July and the Allies were eventually able to break out through the south of the city so troops could push on towards Paris. In the meantime the Americans, who had landed further to the west, were successful in capturing the Cherbourg Peninsula.

Above: A road cleared through the town of Villers-Bocage. Troops needed to fill in craters and move rubble left from bombing attacks so the convoys could move further forward.

Opposite: With the church spire still standing defiantly, bulldozers were brought in to clear the town of Aunay-sur-Odon. German troops had deliberately created barriers from the rubble to stop the Allies advancing.

French Resistance lead revolt against the German troops

Opposite: Once the Allies had moved through Normandy they were able to make very good progress towards the capital. This French tank was seen symbolically positioned by the Arc de Triomphe as troops finally reclaimed the capital city. The original plan had been to actually bypass Paris, but members of the resistance began a revolt against the Germans on 20th August, as the Allies crossed the Seine to the north of

the city. The Allied troops therefore moved in to lend their support.

Above: An exhausted soldier catches up with some rest in the Normandy countryside. By the third week in August, fighting had been continuous for ten weeks, most of which was fierce and relentless.

Paris reclaimed

Paris was finally liberated on 25th August 1944. The first to enter the city were the Free French led by General Leclerc. Many of the Germans captured needed police protection from the furious residents of Paris. However, as the celebrations continued the Allies and the French Resistance were working tirelessly to flush out any Germans still in hiding. Around 500 Germans were found in the Chamber of Deputies alone. The well-established supply lines were very quickly able to send in food supplies. Winston Churchill was later granted freedom of the city.

Opposite: Parisians threw themselves to the ground when German snipers fired at General de Gaulle when he arrived for a Thanksgiving Service at Notre Dame. The snipers had remained hidden for three days.

Above: The American GIs marching along the Champs Élysées.

German soldiers captured

Even in the first two days of the invasion, the Allies had begun to take prisoners and those captured would be taken back to the coast. The supply ships still unloading further troops and weapons would then transport them to detention camps in Britain.

Above: A French woman curses a German soldier as he is marched through the streets of St-Mihiel at gunpoint.

Opposite: A captured German prisoner in Brest handed over a 'safe conduct' leaflet to Lt W.F. Kinney. These pamphlets were dropped over the enemy lines and guaranteed good treatment for German soldiers who were willing to surrender.

Second front opened in France

A second front in southern France was opened on 15th August when the US Seventh Army stormed the beaches near Cannes. The French Army B and the French Resistance assisted them as Operation Dragoon began. During the night six battleships and 21 cruisers took the Germans totally by surprise and five thousand tons of bombs were dropped on coastal gun sites. They were met with very little resistance and the following day Hitler uncharacteristically ordered a gradual withdrawal of troops in a line starting at Sens, cutting through Dijon going as far as the Swiss border.

Opposite: With the spire of Rouen Cathedral still standing, the Tricolore was flying above the remains of the city.

Above: Allied paratroopers ready themselves prior to take-off on a mission to Holland, still occupied by the Germans in September 1944.

Brussels liberated

By September the Allies had reached Belgium and Brussels was finally liberated by Canadian troops in the middle of the month. A few days later the port of Antwerp was also recaptured. The Belgians had a resistance movement called the White Army which was to play an essential part with the Allies in the country's liberation. The Americans then marched on towards Germany.

Above: Scenes of joy as the Belgian Brigade, an independent infantry brigade founded in Britain, enters Brussels.

Opposite: US troops clearing possessions from the German homes that had been set alight by Nazi incendiaries.

Italian Front

At the end of August 1944 the Eighth Army began advancing on Italy and by 21st September, Canadian and Greek troops had liberated Rimini having finally pierced the Gothic Line. The Germans put up fierce resistance and the campaign virtually came to halt in the north of the country as the winter set in. Finally in April 1945 a major offensive was launched and Bologna was taken on 21st April. Milan fell four days later and on 29th April senior German officers signed the document giving their unconditional surrender – this took effect from 2nd May.

Above: Italian patriots searching for any remaining Italian or German troops.

Opposite: A shell explodes next to a soldier near Arnhem who miraculously survived.

Germans surrender Aachen

In September 1944 the Allies gradually moved further east and the Germans finally surrendered the town of Aachen, just over the Belgian border, after a ten-day siege. The intensive fighting took place at very close quarters from house to house. Finally the garrison commander Col. Gerhardt Wilck sent two captured American soldiers with a message to the Allied headquarters to negotiate German surrender; the garrison of over sixteen thousand men had completely run out of food, water and ammunition.

Opposite: German troops captured at Aachen surrender to Allied soldiers.

Above: The long line of German troops was then filed out of Aachen.

'Operation Market Garden'

In September 1944 Montgomery launched 'Operation Market Garden'. The main obstacle to advancing through Germany was the Rhine and so he planned to seize important bridgeheads by using gliders and parachute drops to capture Dutch bridges near the German border and to bypass the Siegfried Line. The Americans were to seize bridges across the Maas and the Waal while British paratroopers were dropped at Arnhem to capture two Lower Rhine bridges. It was initially successful with the 1st Parachute Reconnaissance Squadron landing without opposition. However, when the 1st Airborne Division landed forty-five minutes later, the greetings from the delighted Dutch impeded their progress and the Germans were already blowing up one of the bridges.

They then encountered fierce German resistance at Arnhem and the supply of further troops was held up by disruption to radio links. The Germans then intercepted the plans for the operation. The whole mission was dogged by misfortune and casualties were high. Eventually after ten days, Montgomery ordered troops to withdraw with the loss of 1,200 lives and a further 6,642 taken prisoner.

Opposite: British troops move rapidly through the Dutch town of Flushing, on the lookout for enemy snipers.

Above: Gelsenkirchen is finally entered by British and American tank crews.

German counter-attacks

Despite the fact that by mid-1944, it was clear that the Germans would be defeated, Hitler refused to give in, believing that new weapons would turn the tide of the war. The V1 pilotless flying bomb, or 'Doodlebug' had been developed. These weapons were initially launched from a site in Calais; they were designed to fly across the Channel and then cut out when over London. It then took 15 seconds for the bombs to fall silently containing nearly a ton of explosive, potentially causing damage over a quarter-of-a-mile radius. The first of these landed in London in June and in the first two weeks over 1,700 people were killed, leading to another huge wave of evacuation. Gradually the threat lessened as British defence techniques against them improved, destroying over half before they reached their target.

The sites in northern France were also becoming overrun as the Allies began to advance into France. In September, a second weapon, the V2, was deployed, a long-range rocket that was being launched from sites still under German control. The first landed in Chiswick leaving a massive crater and killing three people. The impact of the V2 was far greater, it was fast and no warning was given. One of the worst attacks was on Woolworths in November when 160 were killed and 200 injured. The store was completely flattened. In December the Germans attacked Antwerp and in one hit on a cinema, 567 were killed.
Opposite: The carnage left in a Belgian town after a German counter-attack.
Above: Refugees in Belgium heading for the safety of the Allied lines.

Battle of the Bulge

The last major confrontation between the Allies and the Germans became known as the Battle of the Bulge and lasted for six weeks. The Germans planned to split the Allied line, capture Antwerp and then sweep north to surround and take out four Allied armies. Hitler believed this would force the Western Allies into peace negotiations favouring the Axis powers. More than a million troops took part in fierce fighting in very poor weather conditions with the January being the coldest on record. The fighting centred on the Ardennes area and was spread over sixty miles of Allied front with the Belgian town of Bastogne bearing the brunt of the offensive. Ultimately there were over 140,000 casualties and although the Germans managed to create 'bulges' in the Allied line their mission was unsuccessful. It also depleted some of the German army and reduced their supplies which made it easier for the Allies to make the final assault in the following month. It was during this offensive that the US commander Tony McAuliffe, after a request to surrender, famously replied 'Aw, nuts!'

Above: German soldiers left for dead in the snow. They had been shot by machine gun fire as they tried to overrun a command post at Bastogne.

Opposite: British troops searching for snipers at Blerick on the River Maas. This was the end of the German bridgehead on the western bank.

Defeat inevitable

By the beginning of 1945 German resistance was crumbling fast and German defeat was clearly imminent. During January the Russians marched through Germany from the east and successfully liberated the concentration camp at Auschwitz on 27th. The Allied armies continued to push through the Rhineland and finally, on 7th March, the Americans captured the bridge at Remegen which gave the Allies a much-needed crossing point. Others were soon established so troops could quickly move further into Germany. On 4th February Churchill, Stalin and Roosevelt met at Yalta to initiate discussions about the division of Germany after the war.

Opposite: Churchill when visiting the Command HQ at Jülich crosses a Bailey bridge over the Roer commenting, 'After the magnificent job your troops did getting across, it will be an honour to walk its length'.

Above: Men and supplies crossing the Rhine. Many bridges were built and this particular one was already in use the day after the Allies crossed the river.

YOU ARE NO
CROSSING T
RHINE RIVE
THROUGH COUR
OF 'E' CO. 17 A
ENGR. BN. AN
'C' CO. 202
ENGR. C. BN

Building bridges

Above: A pontoon bridge across the Rhine was constructed in a mere 6.5 hours. These temporary bridges were supported by floating pontoons that provided enough buoyancy to support the bridge and subsequent loads. They were temporary structures that could be destroyed afterwards or dismantled and then carried.

Opposite: US 7th Army Infantrymen provide cover from the western bank as Allies cross the river under fire from Germans sited on the east bank.

German soldiers captured

Above: Two wounded German soldiers were successfully captured by the British after a battle at Millingen when Montgomery's troops had fought to keep control of a bridgehead.

Opposite: One of the youngest Germans ever captured by the British. Not yet fifteen years old, he was taken in March when the Siegfried Line was attacked.

RAF deploys troops in the air

While troops crossed bridges over the Rhine at the end of March, military action was not restricted to the ground. A total of 40,000 paratroopers of the First Airborne Division were dropped onto the eastern bank from the C-47 transport carriers. The RAF deployed thousands of airborne troops to attack the Germans positioned to the east of the river. One particular air fleet stretching for 500 miles took in thousands of paratroopers and towed gliders into battle.

Opposite: British troops move on past the eastern banks of the Rhine, passing the bodies of German soldiers.
Above: A long line taken prisoner by General Patton's men.

Hitler commits suicide

The Russian armies had marched through Germany from the east and encircled Berlin by 25th April 1945. After five days of fierce fighting, which left more than 100,000 Germans dead, the garrison finally fell and Hitler and Eva Braun, his bride of 36 hours, committed suicide.

Above: An American soldier guards German detainees.
Opposite: British and Canadian troops eventually capture Emmerich in early April under Montgomery's command.

Prisoner of War camps

Above: British POWs at Stalag 11B just south of Fallingbostel. They were first British POWs to be freed and were clearly suffering from malnutrition.

Opposite: 18,000 POWs waiting for release from Altengrabow Camp.

Concentration camps

Above: The concentration camp at Belsen was found and liberated in April. There were 60,000 people crammed into the camp, most suffering from dysentery, typhus and typhoid. The Allies rushed medical teams in but it was too late for many. An estimated 10,000 bodies were lying around the camp when it was liberated. Belsen and other similar camps were set up by the Nazi regime which sought to incarcerate those people it believed polluted the Aryan purity of Germany. The camps also became a focal part of Hitler's 'Final Solution' where genocide was used to eliminate the Jewish race in Nazi-occupied territory.

Opposite: In the last few weeks of the war German guerrilla groups known as werewolves had become apparent behind Allied lines. They were never very effective as their numbers were few and their action came too late in the war. This member was soon detained.

VE Day

The news of Germany's unconditional surrender was declared on 7th May 1945 at General Eisenhower's HQ in Rheims. It would take effect at midnight on 8th May and was to be celebrated as Victory in Europe Day (VE Day). It was then ratified in Berlin on 9th with the Russian Marshal Zhukov and Eisenhower's deputy Air Chief Marshal Tedder, signing on behalf of the Allies.

Above: Celebratory street parties were held all over Britain.
Opposite: The ruins of Berlin after heavy bombing raids. These were carried out just before the Allies attacked the city from the ground.

Celebration!

Opposite: A family celebrates in Salisbury Square, showing V for Victory signs and Union Jacks. The streamers were made from tickertape.

Above: An Oxford Street vendor taking advantage of the mass jubilation selling Union Jacks from his barrow.

The Royal Family leads the celebrations

Above: Massive crowds gathered outside Buckingham Palace on VE Day as everyone called for the King. He soon appeared with Queen Elizabeth and Princesses Elizabeth and Margaret, who were then joined by Winston Churchill. The two princesses later joined in with the street celebrations. Licensing laws were duly suspended for the night.

A service of thanksgiving was held at St Margaret's Church and attended by Churchill and other Members of Parliament.
Opposite: Crowds gather at Trafalgar Square to listen to Churchill's announcement.

Soldiers return

Above: A British sergeant returns to a Devon village after his release from a POW camp to be greeted jubilantly by his wife and son.

Opposite: Celebrations in London.

Conditions in Germany

Above: By May 1945 rationing in Germany was so meagre that many were starving. Those willing to work were paid well and were able to supplement their rations. This was particularly true of those willing to work in the heavy construction industry as they began to rebuild the cities. Women were employed in human chains clearing rubble.

Opposite: Children's VE Day party at Brockley in South London.

Potsdam conference

Above: President Roosevelt had died on 12th April, only a month away from Germany's surrender. Vice-president Truman was immediately sworn in as President and met Churchill in July at Potsdam along with Russian representatives to go over the final details of the peace process.

Opposite: Churchill met British military commanders at Berlin airport when he arrived for the Potsdam conference. Immediately after VE Day, the coalition government had been dissolved and a new election called. Labour won a landslide victory against the shocked Tories. Clement Attlee then took over from Churchill at Potsdam where the conference was continuing.

Atomic bombs dropped over Hiroshima and Nagasaki

The Allies bombed Japan from October 1944 to August 1945 while plans for the Allied invasion were formulated, until President Truman finally sanctioned the atomic bomb. The first was dropped from a B-29 bomber onto Hiroshima on 6th August. It burst at around 8.15 am, 2,000 feet in the air and instantly killed thousands of people. The pilot Robert Lewis famously asked his crew, 'My God, what have we done?' Three days later another was dropped over Nagasaki and an estimated 103,000 people died, either immediately or within four months of the bombing. Even today, the health of thousands is still being watched due to the effects of the radiation.

Left: The mushroom-shaped cloud that rose 20,000 feet over Nagasaki.

Opposite: The complete devastation caused to the city.

Japan surrenders

On 14th August 1945, Emperor Hirohito finally offered his unconditional surrender, five days after the second bomb was dropped on Nagasaki. As this signified the final end to the war, celebrations again lasted well into the night: the war had lasted twenty days short of six very long years, although people were shocked by the devastating atomic bombs that led to its conclusion.

Above: A London policeman is held aloft during the celebrations by some US and New Zealand military.

Opposite: The destruction left behind at Hiroshima.

VJ Day

Above: Jubilant revellers at Trafalgar Square on VJ Day.

Opposite: Crowds gather at Piccadilly Circus to celebrate the Japanese surrender.

217

Victory Day

More formal celebrations were held on 8th June 1946 to thank everyone for the part they played in the war. A parade stretching for twenty miles contained 21,000 British and Allied forces and many civilian workers.

Opposite: The King and Queen, along with their daughters and Queen Mary watch the 300-strong RAF flypast, during the parade.
Above: Field Marshal Montgomery, now Viscount of Alamein, led the procession of vehicles in the parade as it set off from Clarence Gate, Regent's Park.

Fireworks for Victory

Above: Troops from India took part in the parade. All nations that fought for the Allies were represented.

Opposite: A huge firework display over the Thames ended the day as fireworks were launched from barges moored up on the Thames.

The Nuremberg Trials

Above: November 1945 saw the start of months of trials of the Nazi leadership as war criminals. Twenty-one were on trial with three eventually acquitted, seven receiving prison sentences and eleven sentenced to death. They were hanged on 16th October 1946. One of the eleven was Hermann Goering who avoided execution by swallowing a cyanide pill he had concealed throughout the trial.

Opposite: The Houses of Parliament silhouetted during a celebratory firework display.